I CAN DRAW PETS!

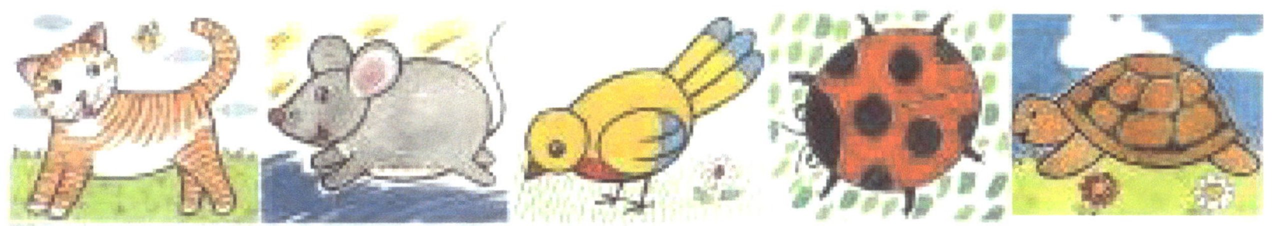

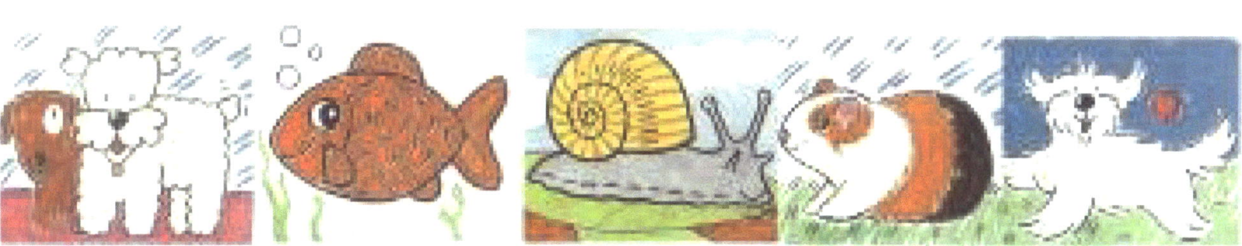

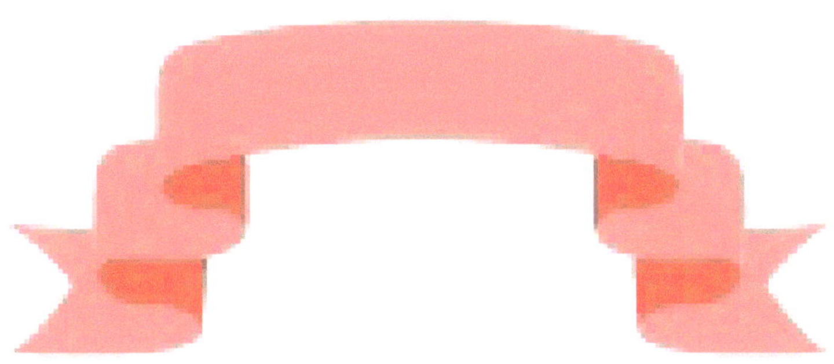

The Cat

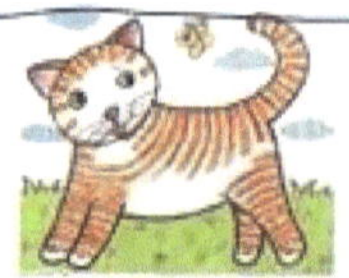

One round, then two ears, it's not complicated. Be careful, apply yourself to make the muzzle!Is he asleep or curious? Take a good look at his eyes.From the back, it's easier.

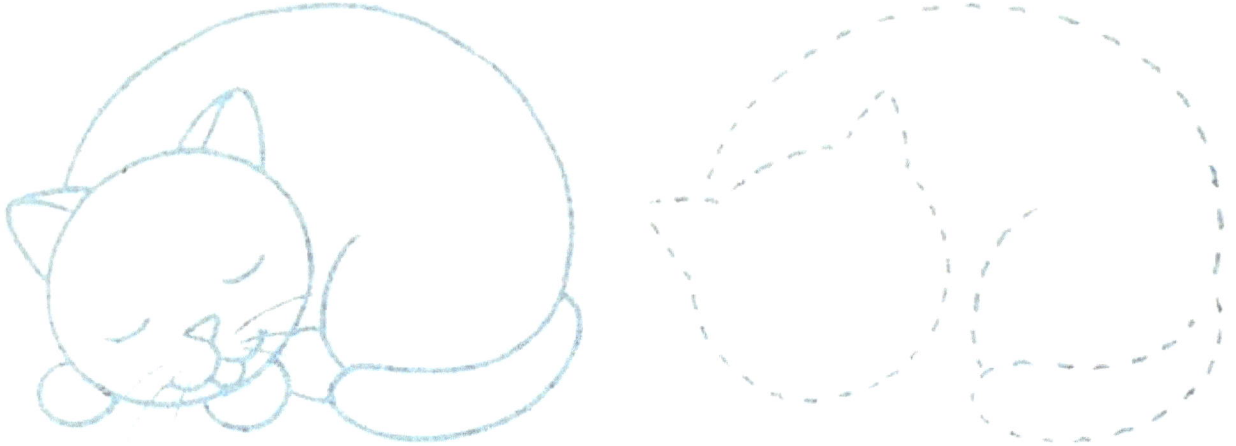

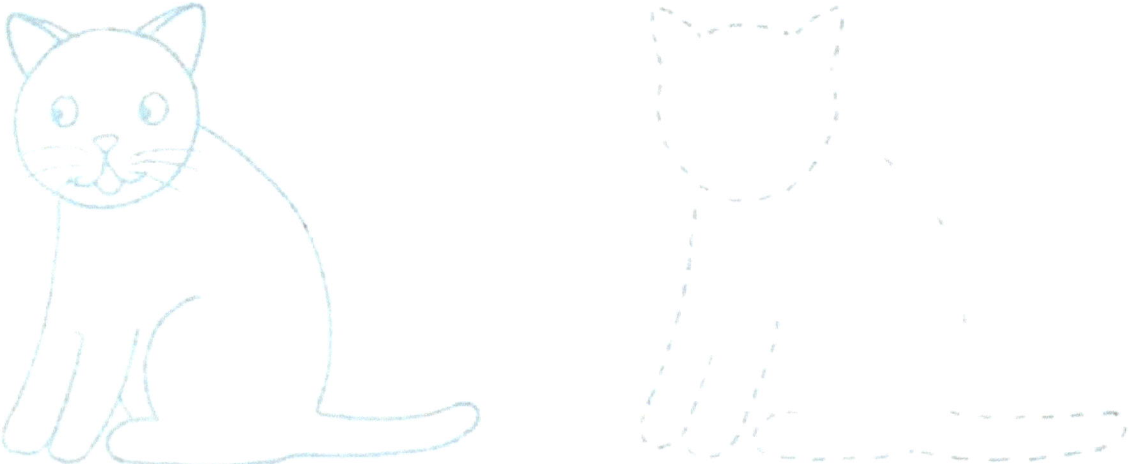

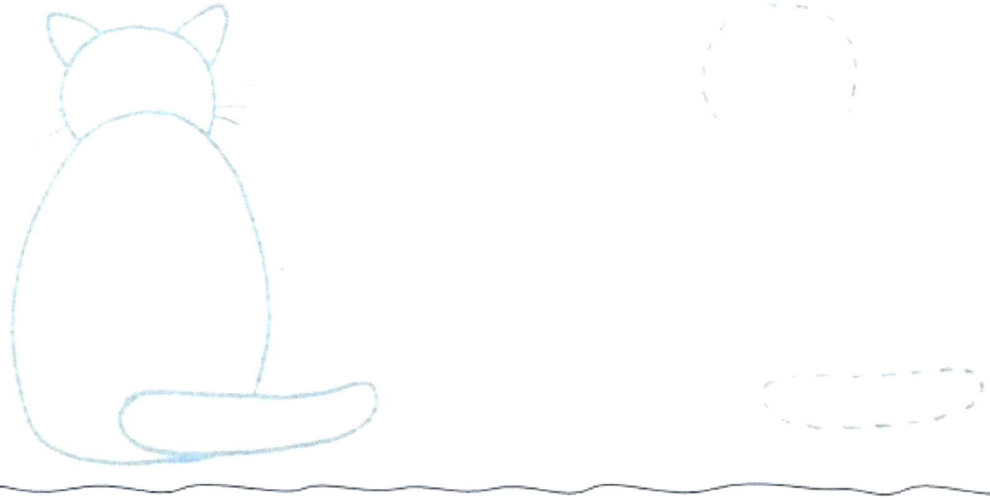

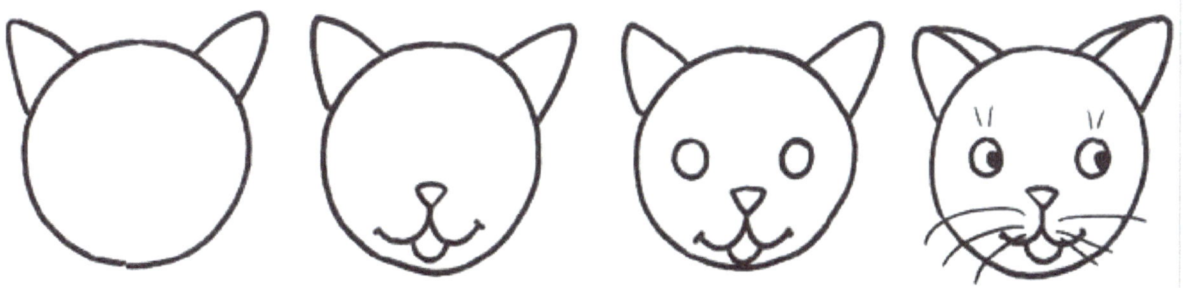

With colored pencils, it will be easier to make him a nice striped sweater.Choose the tones you want.

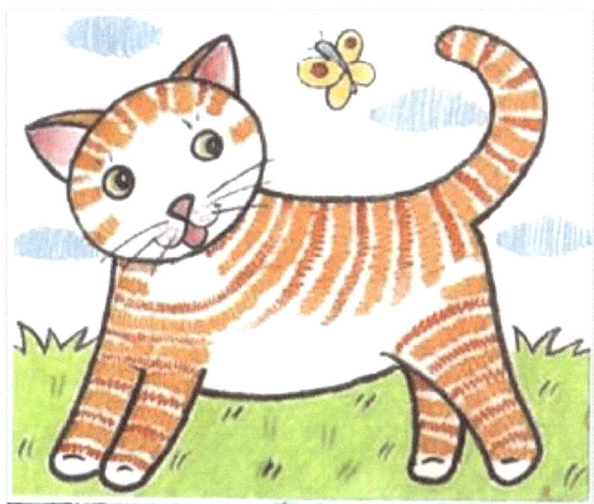

Trace over the blue lines of each model and then complete the drawing.

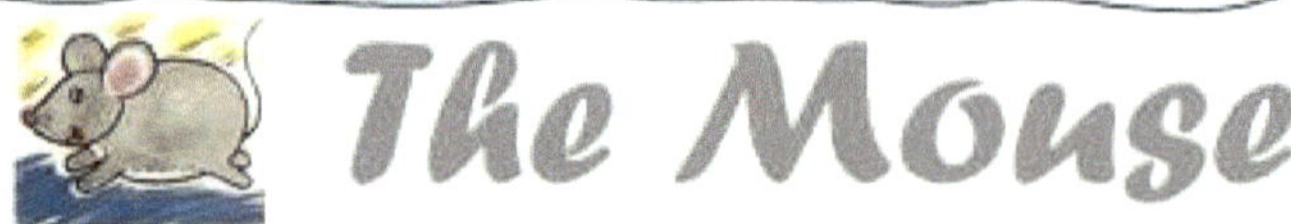 # The Mouse

On the left, on the right, it runs, with its small legs! Worried or happy? All you have to do is change the direction of her mouth, without forgetting its whiskers.

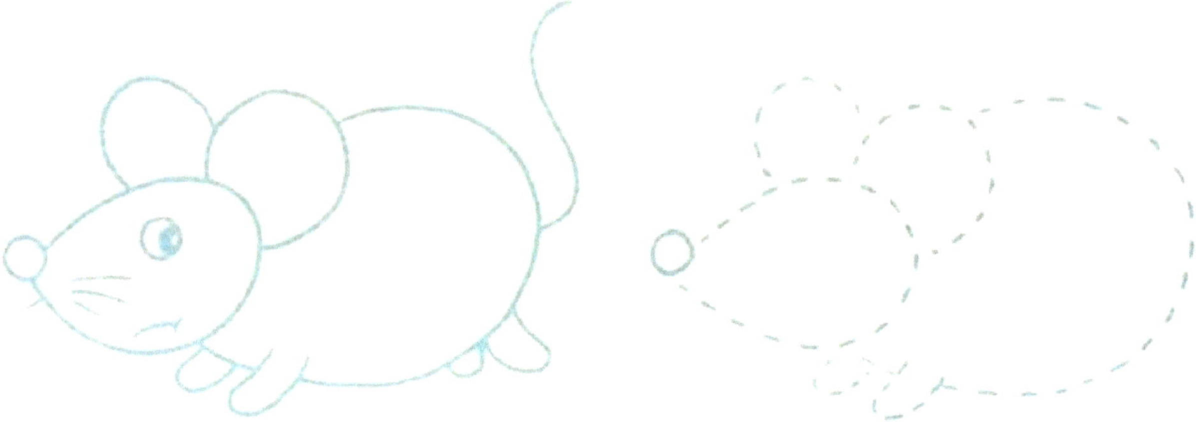

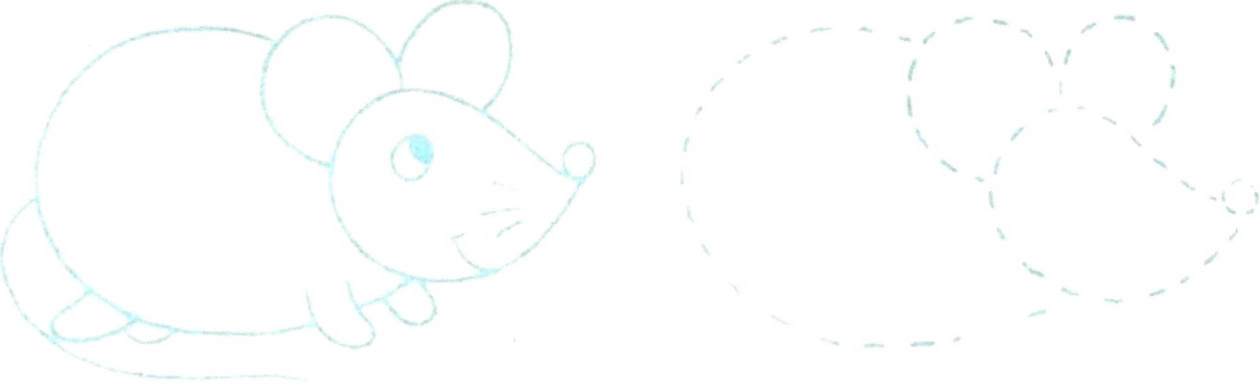

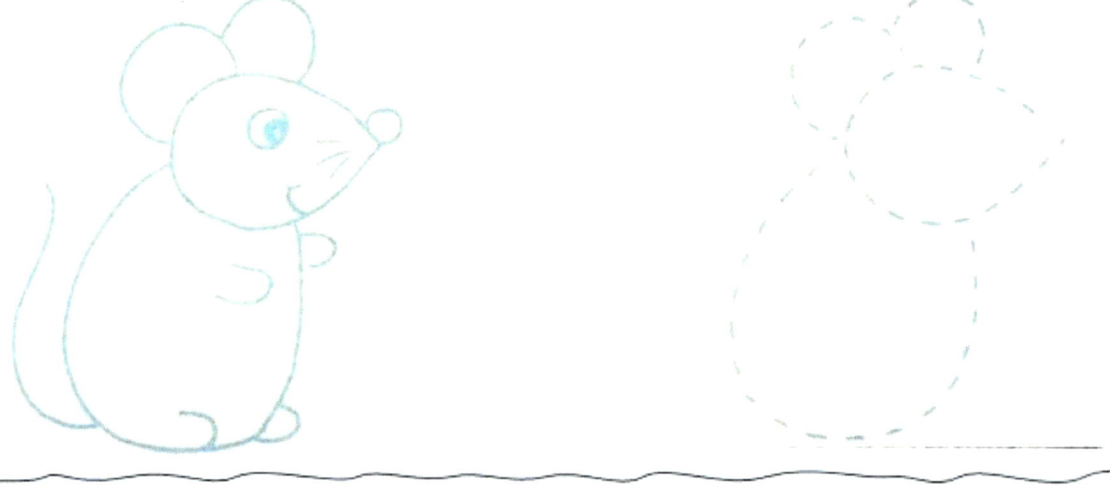

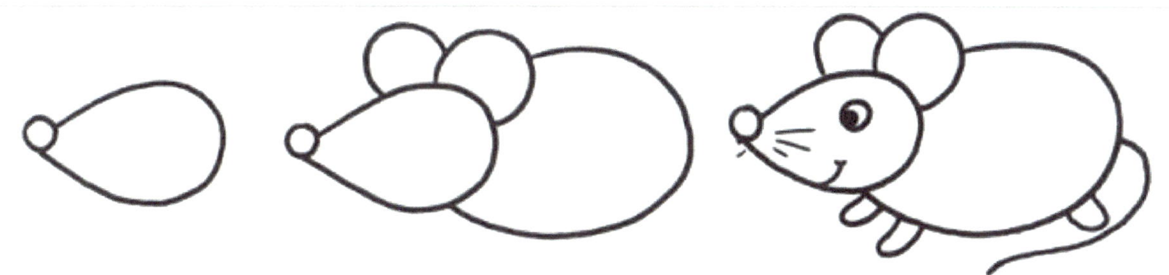

Beware, it runs very fast! So, color it with pastels or paint, it will be faster.

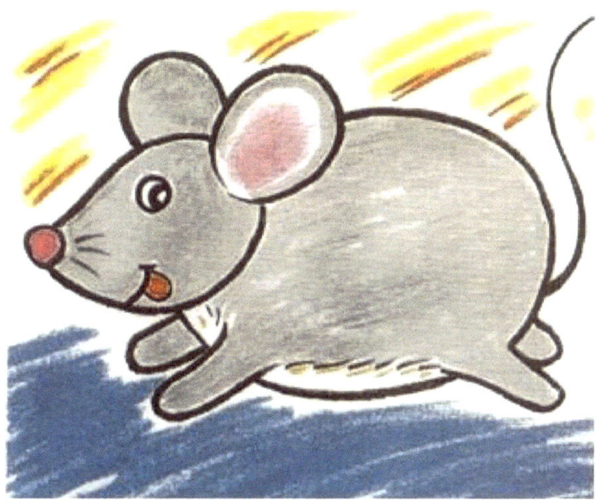

 **Trace over the blue lines of each model and then complete the drawing.**

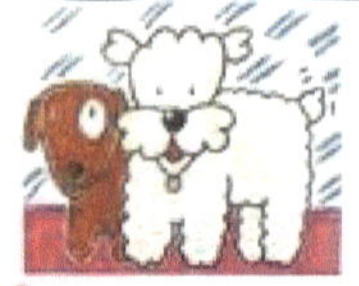

Little Dogs

Two dots for the eyes, a bigger one for the nose. Then it's just a question of hair and length. Two small strokes on each side of the tip of the tail and the little dog looks happy!

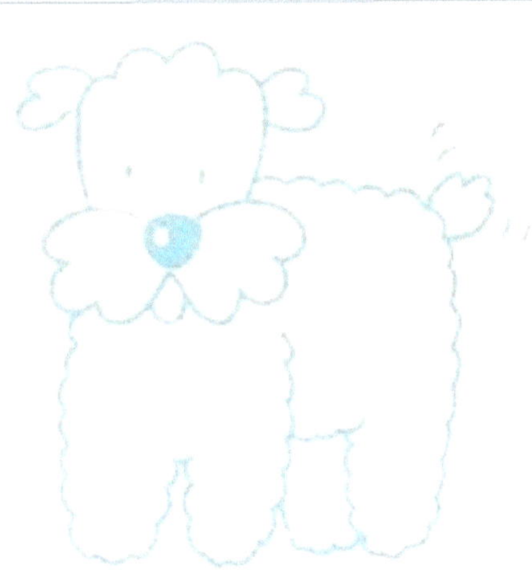

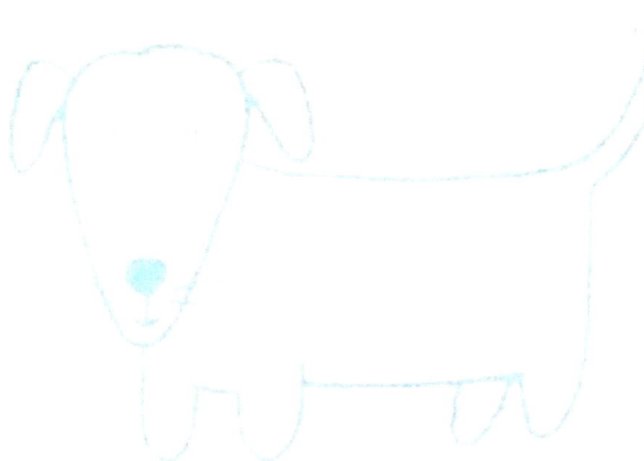

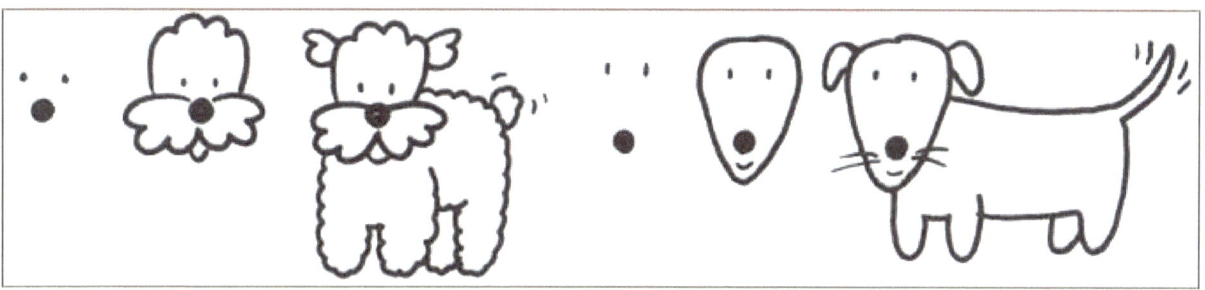

Complete the outline of the two little dogs, without forgetting the ears!

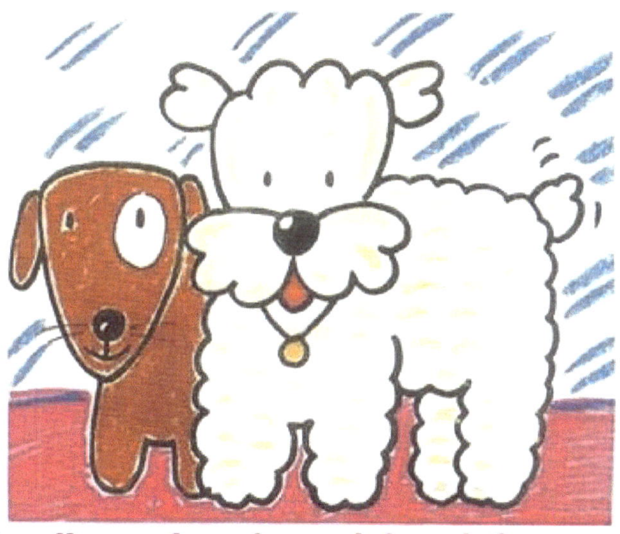

Trace over the blue lines of each model and then complete the drawing.

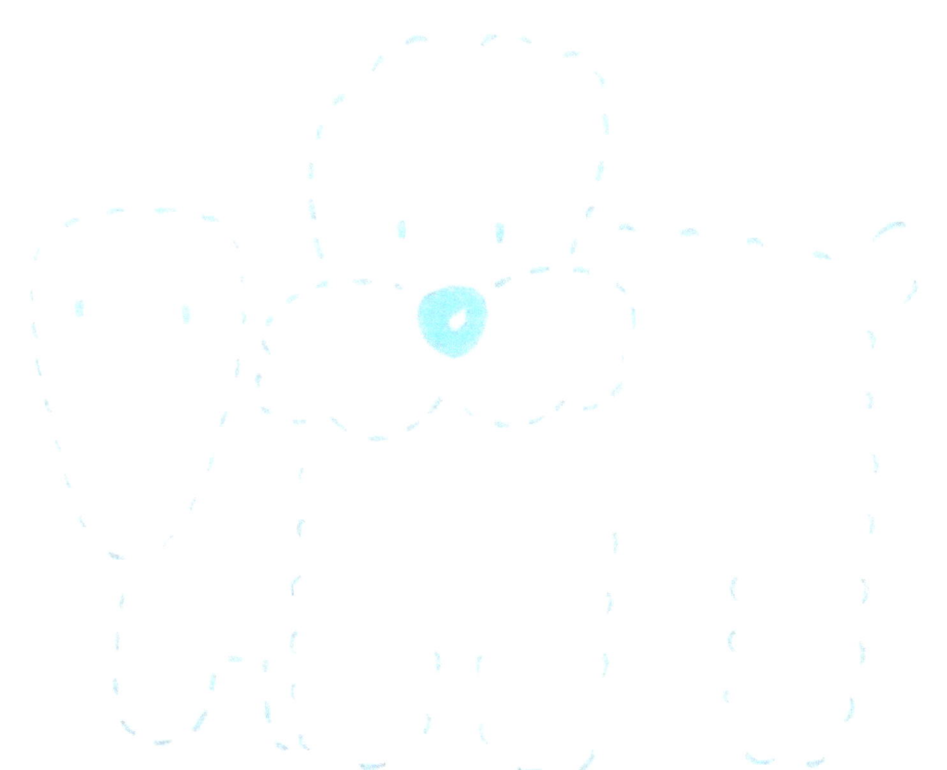

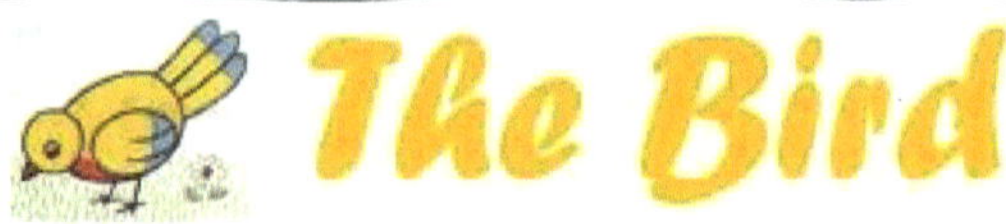 The Bird

Whether it pecks, sings or flies, only the beak and the eye change places. You can decorate its wings and tail by coloring its plumes in different colors.

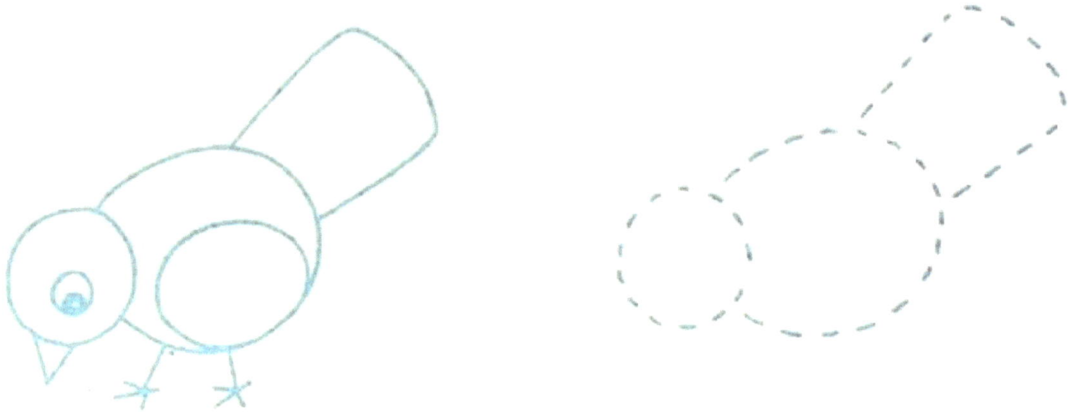

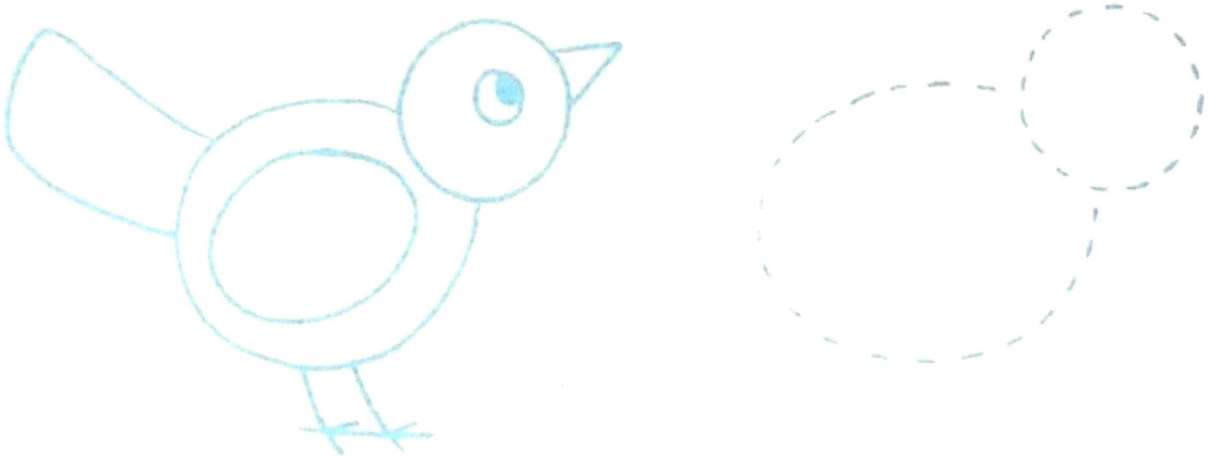

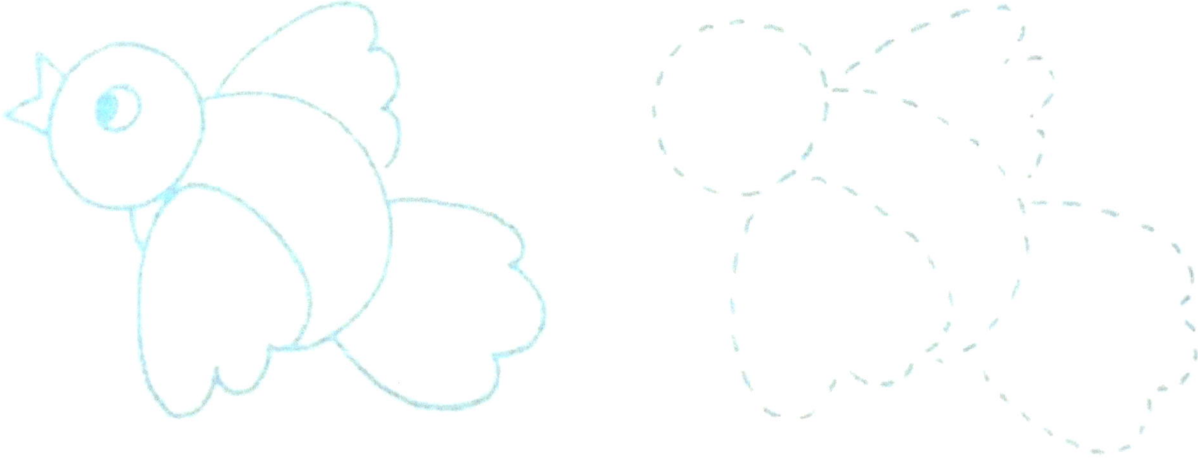

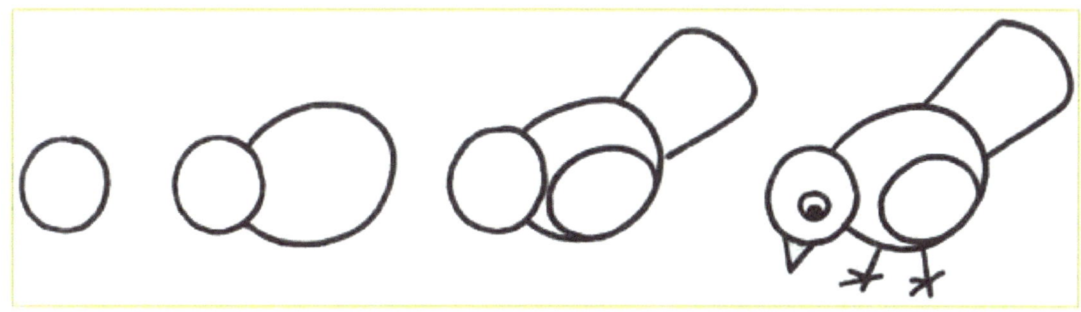

The color of the bird may vary. The model is made with large felt-tip pens.

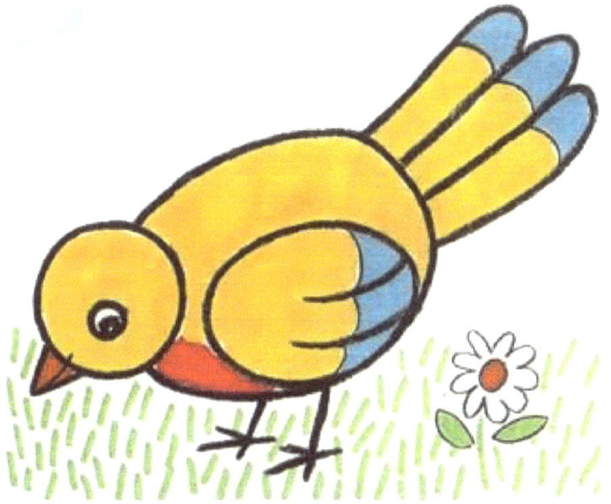

 Trace over the blue lines of each model and then complete the drawing.

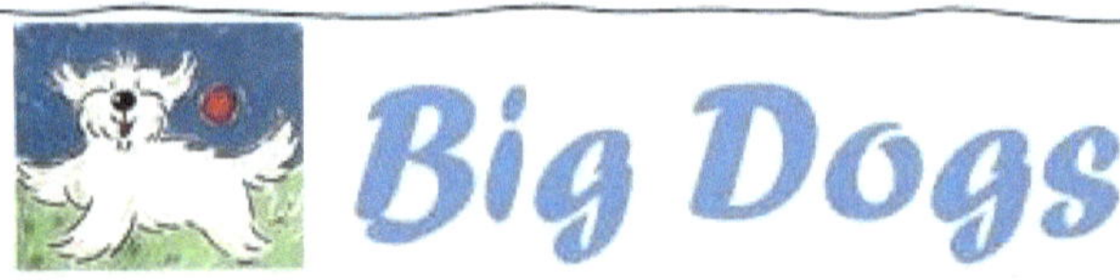

Big Dogs

It's like the little dogs, but observe the differences well. You can give them a wide variety of expressions just with eyes and ears.

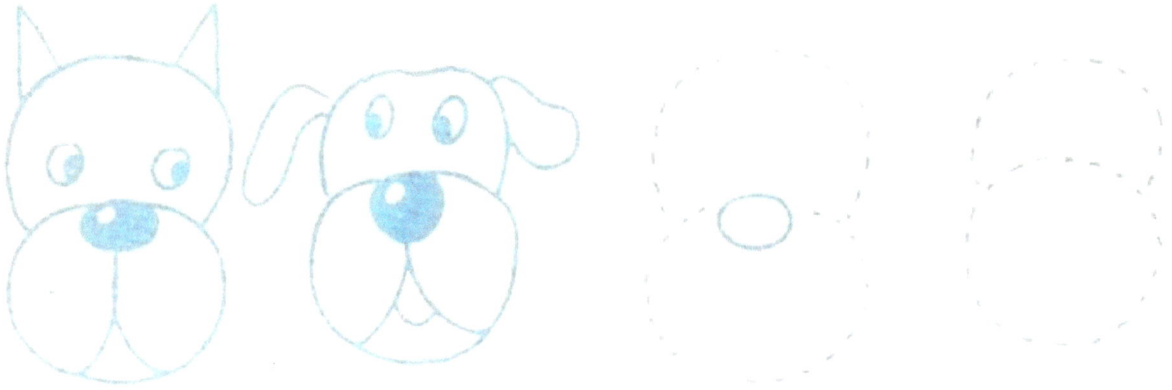

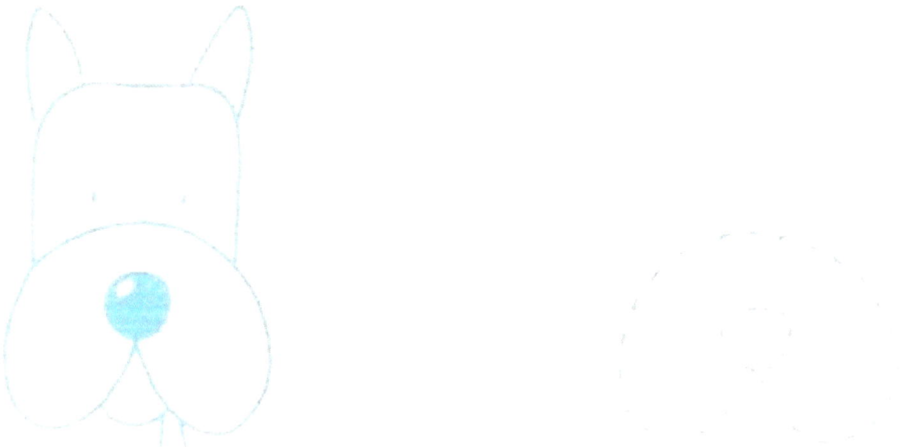

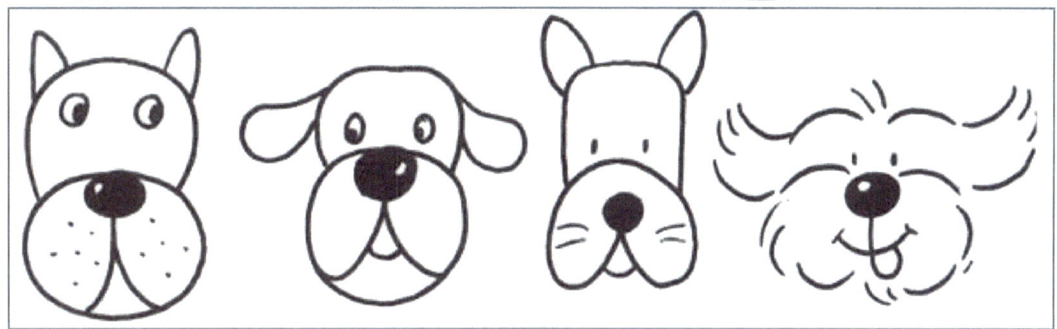

**Make quick strokes with a black felt pen to create movement.
Use pastels for the rest of the body.**

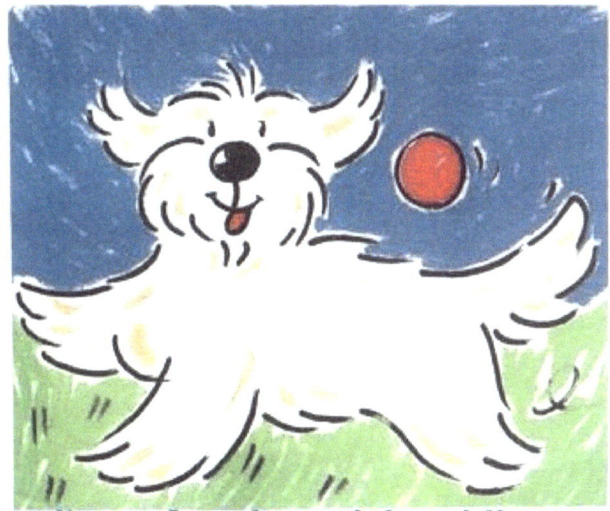

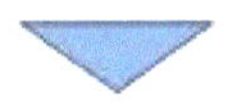 **Trace over the blue lines of each model and then complete the drawing.**

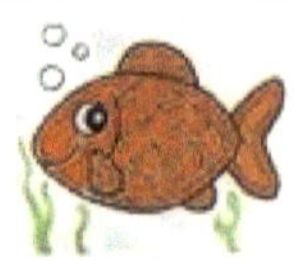

The Fish

Round fish or long fish, the fins and tail are always in the same
place. In profile or in front, sad, cheerful or with a mischievous
eye: it's up to you!

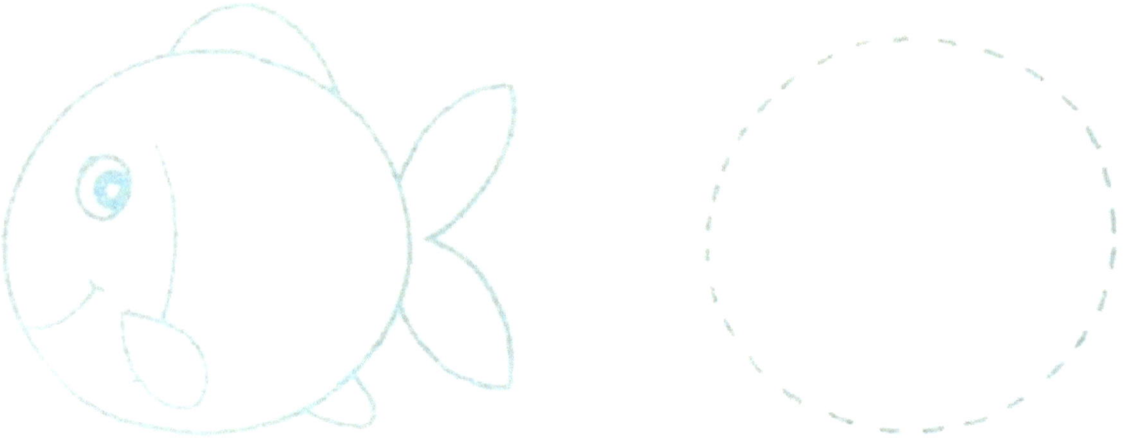

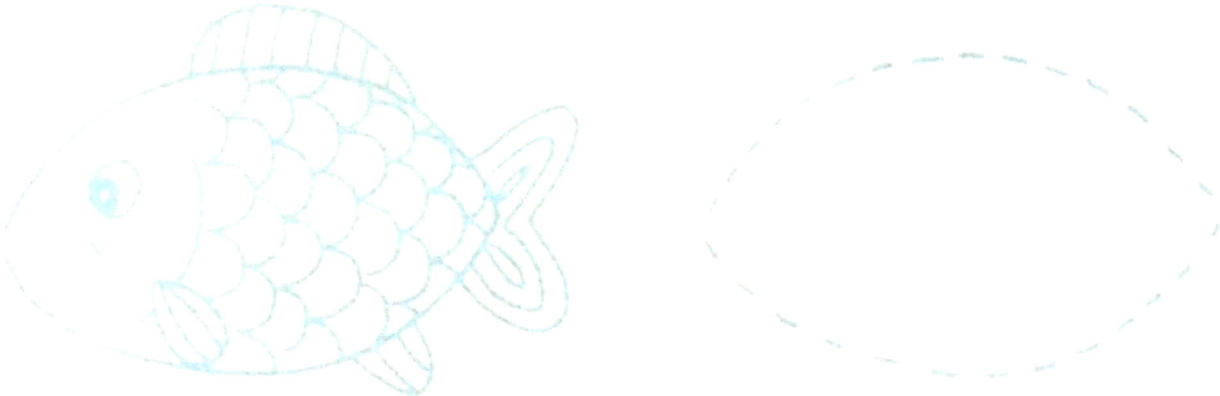

You can color your fish with pastels or felt-tip pens.

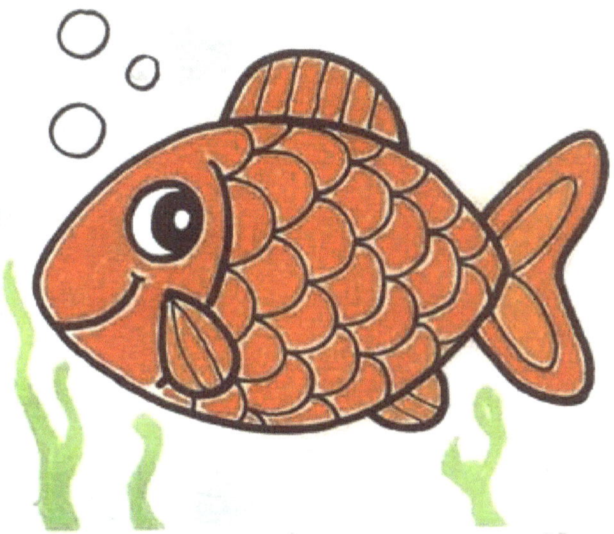

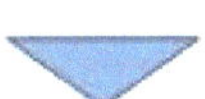 Trace over the blue lines of each model and then complete the drawing.

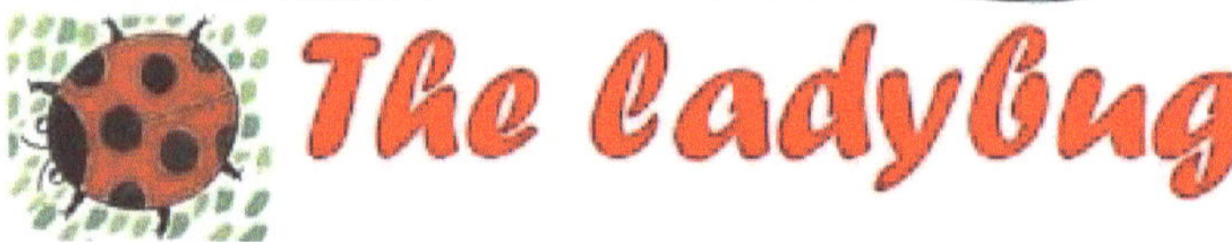

It is easy to draw: a large red circle with a few black dots and six small legs. Here it is ready to fly away!

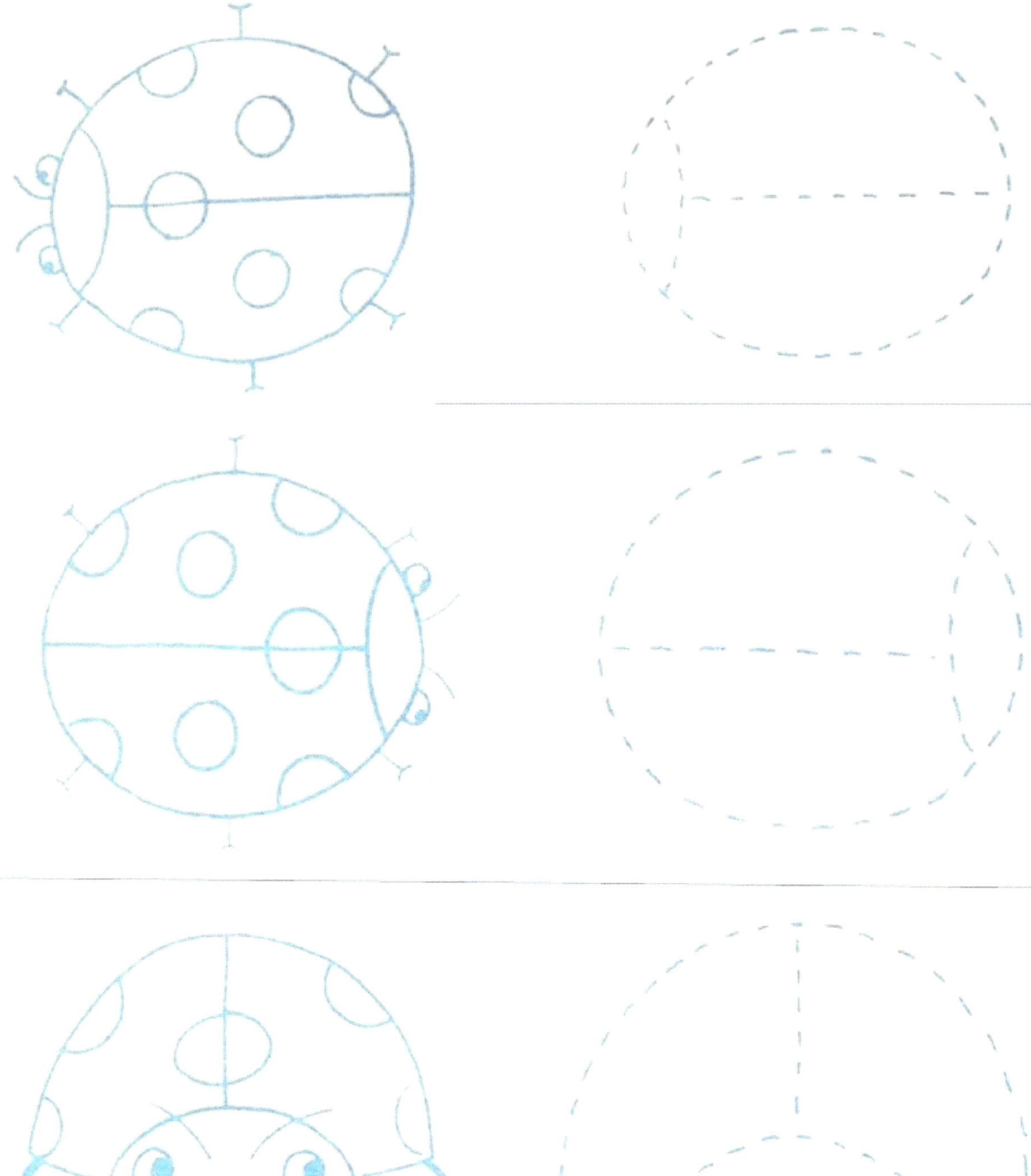

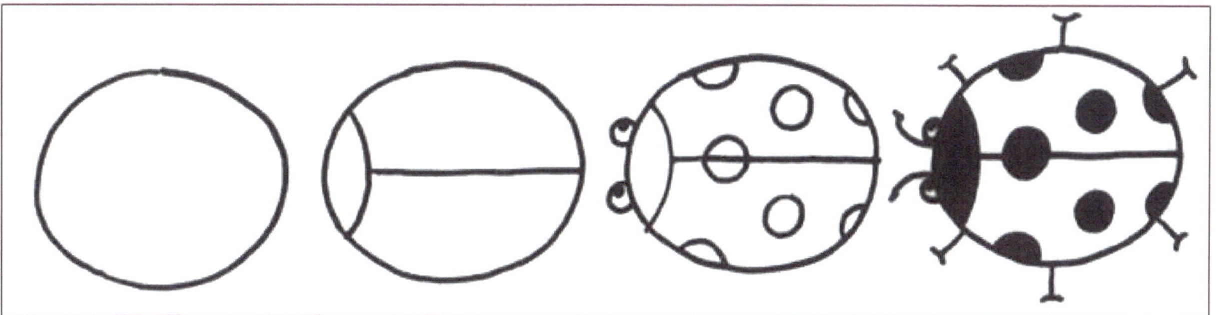

Put a ladybug on your finger and observe how cute it is.

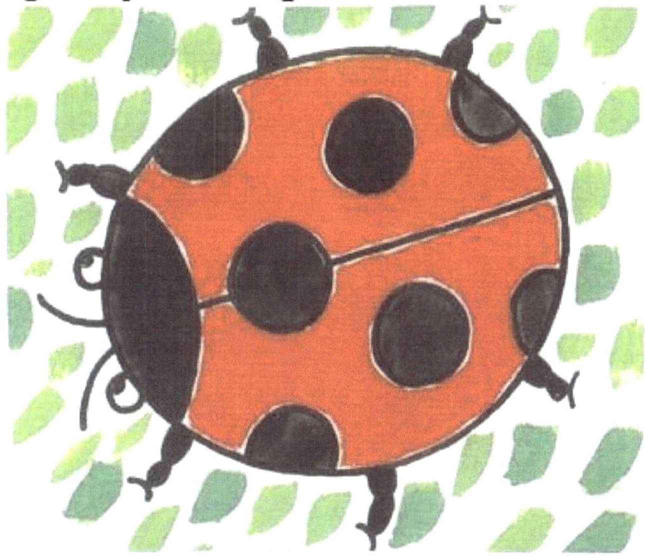

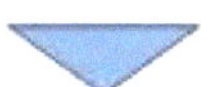 Trace over the blue lines of each model and then complete the drawing.

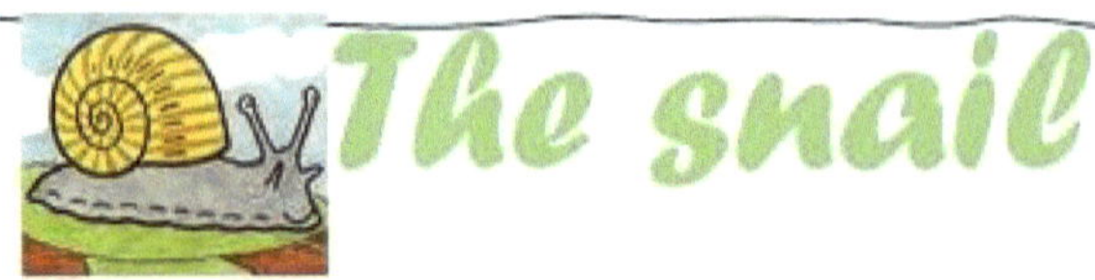

The snail

Th spiral of the shell must start in the direction of the arrow. The snail has four horns and its eyes are at the end of the longest.

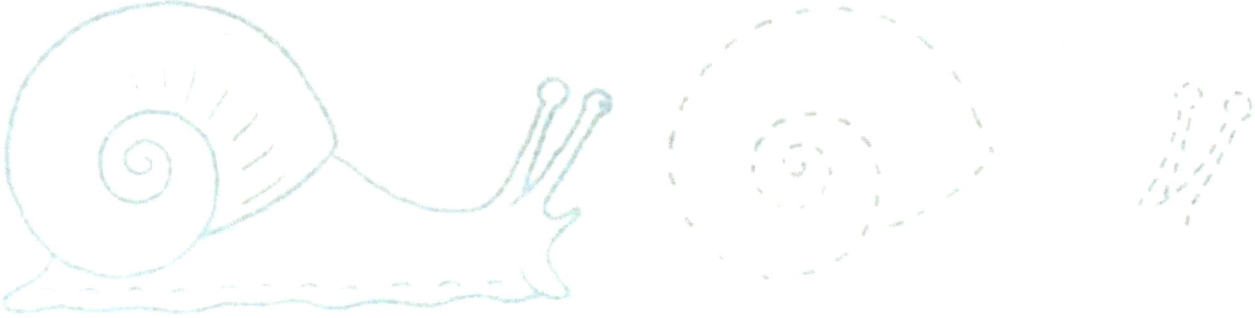

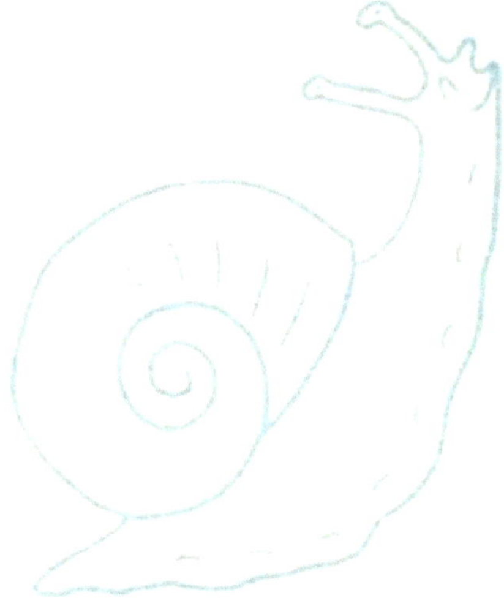

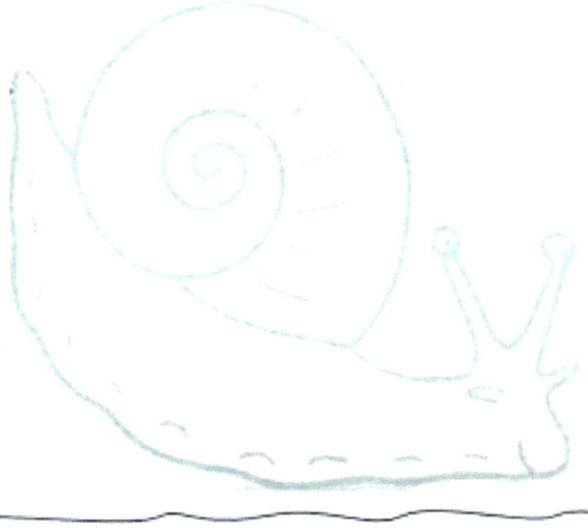

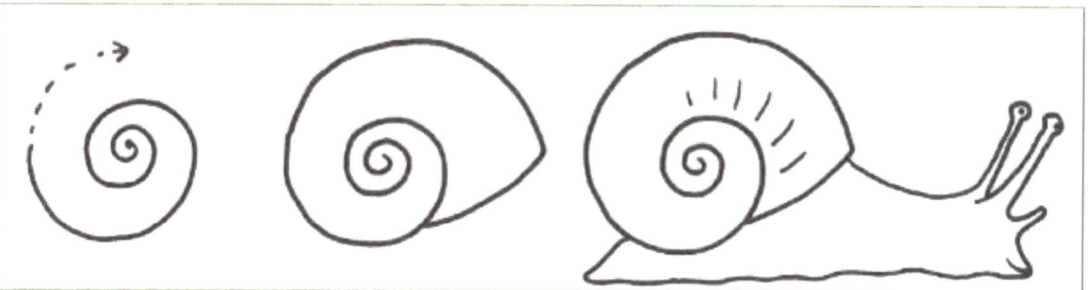

Have fun coloring its shell according to your fantasy. Don't hesitate to put some greenery... It loves it!

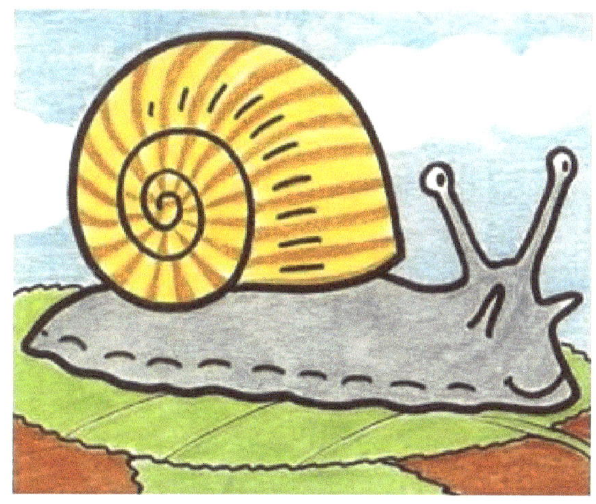

Trace over the blue lines of each model and then complete the drawing.

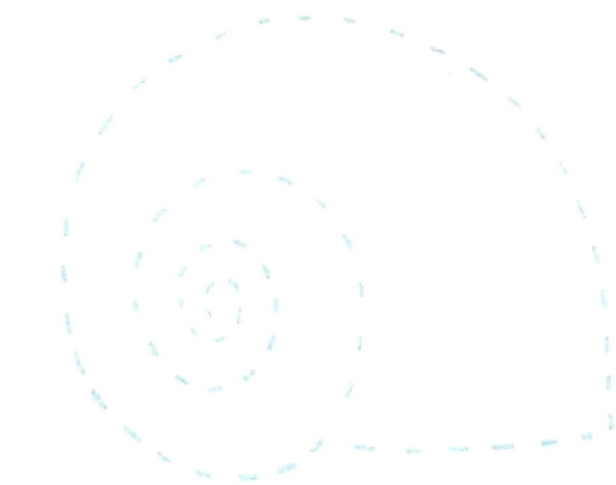

The Guinea pig

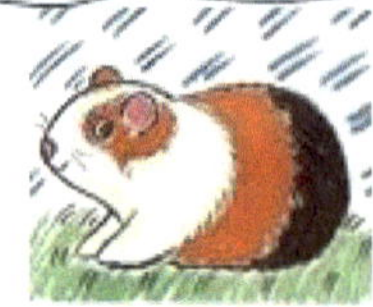

It is not very easy to draw, because it looks like both a rabbit and a mouse. So, observe the shapes well. You can replace the continuous line with lines that imitate its fur.

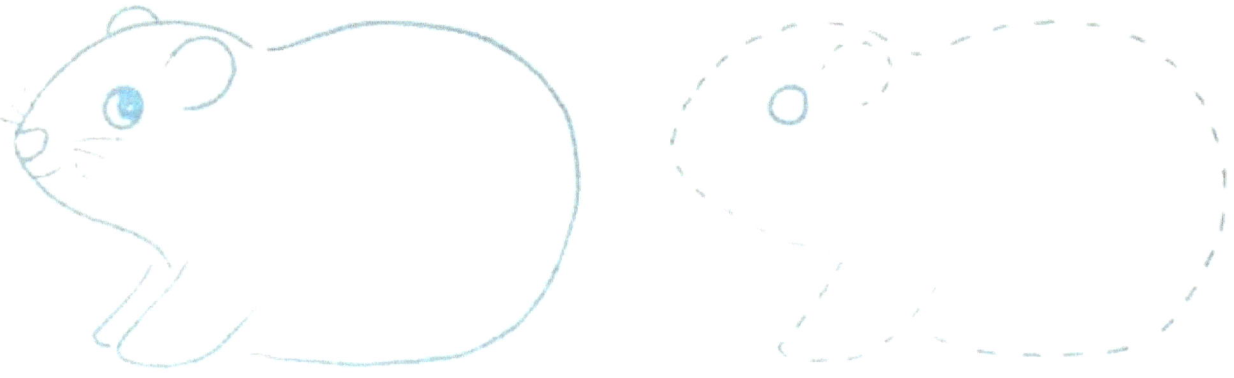

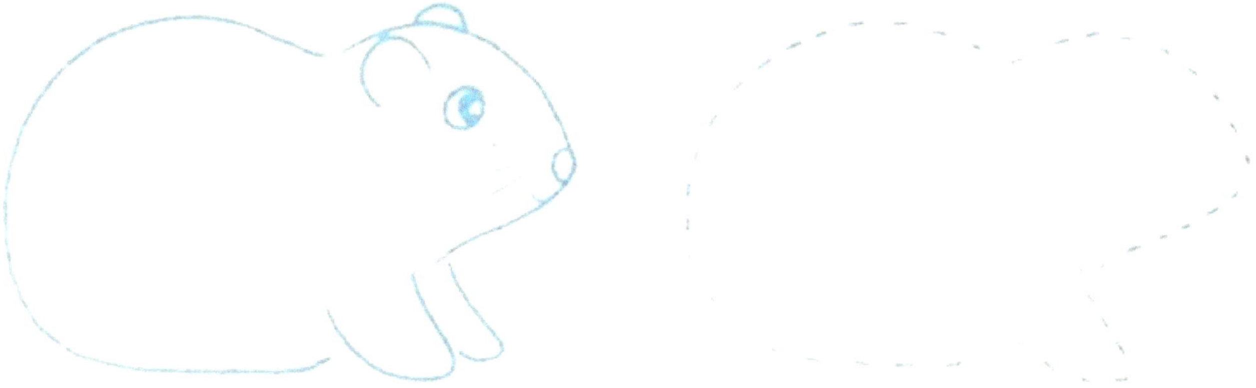

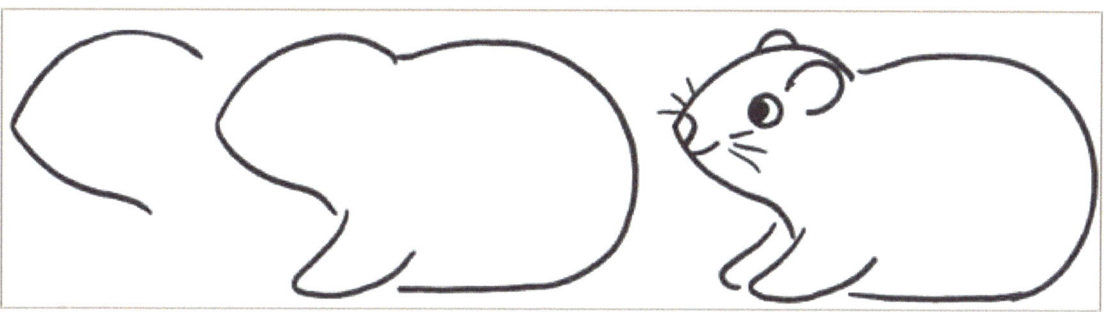

While having fun with dry pastel, brown and orange, invent a new guinea pig.

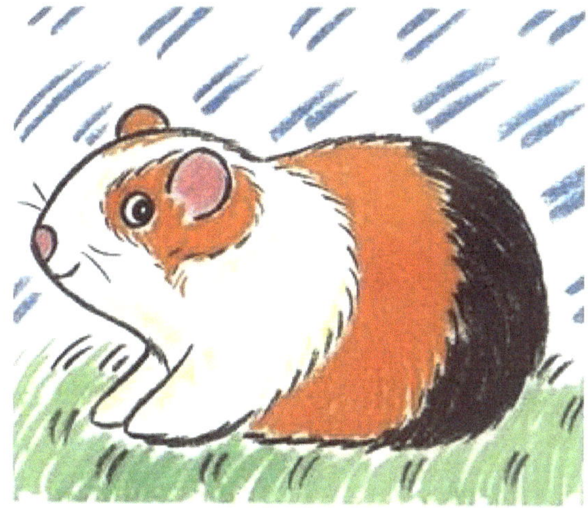

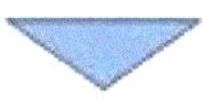
Trace over the blue lines of each model and then complete the drawing.

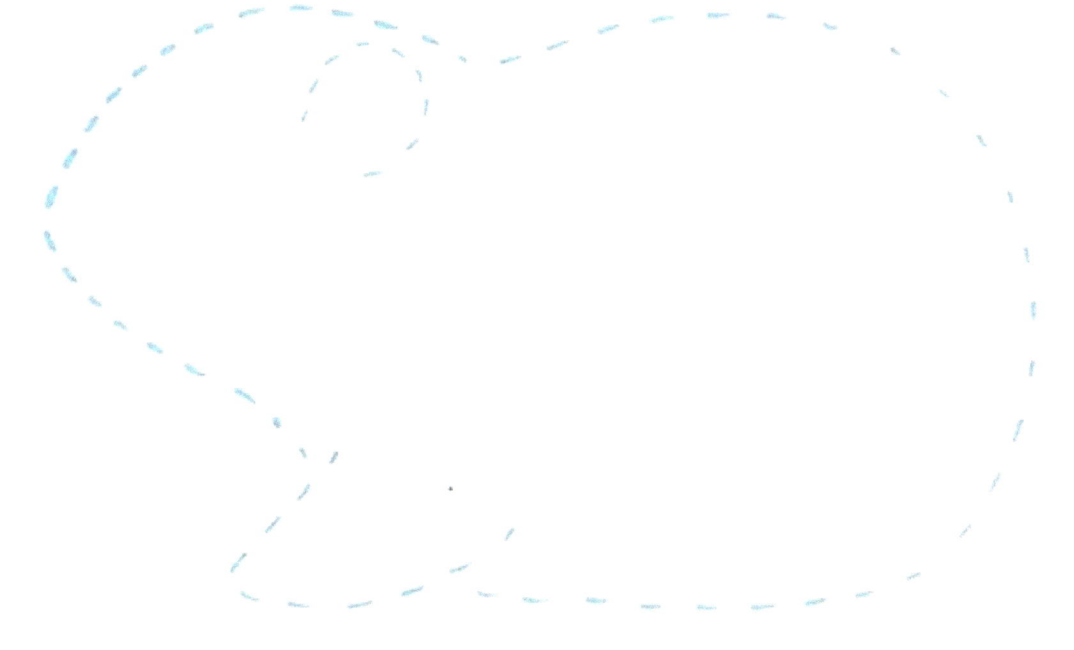

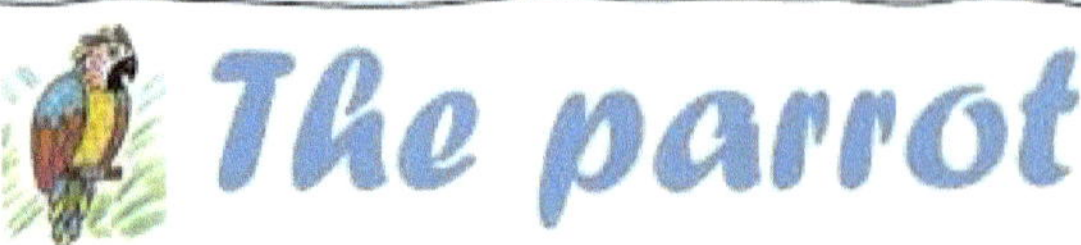 # The parrot

It is quite difficult to draw, although his head is made in a few well-placed strokes. Its plumage can vary according to your imagination. Beware, it always repeats the same thing!

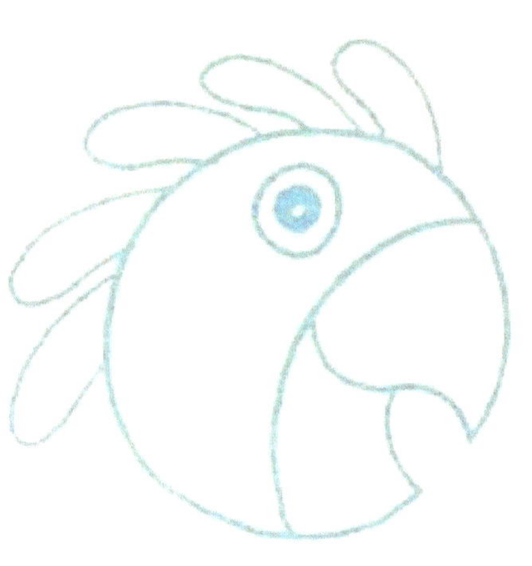

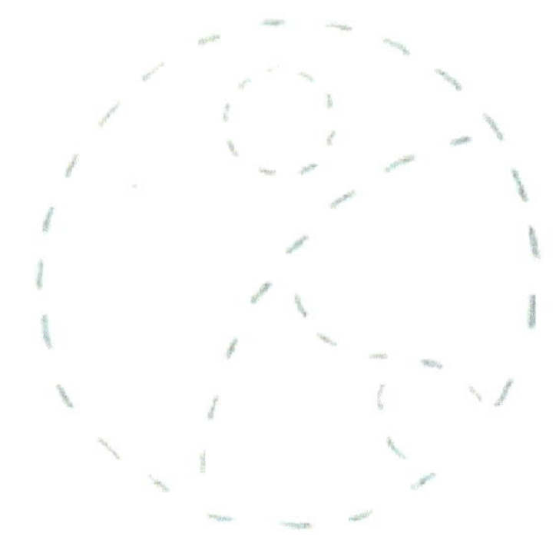

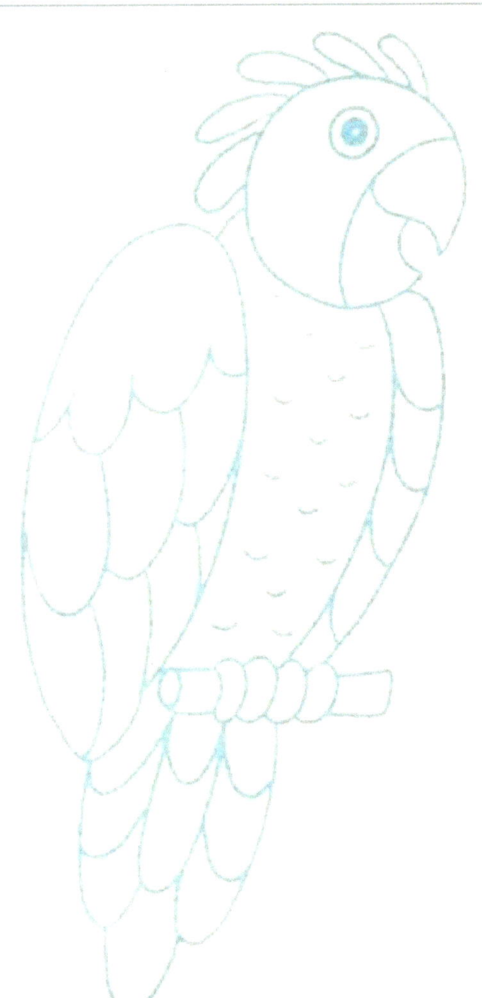

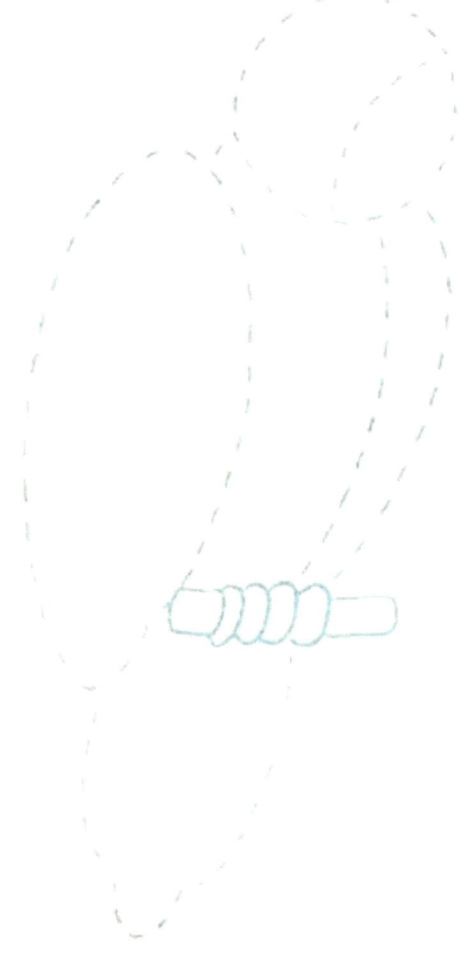

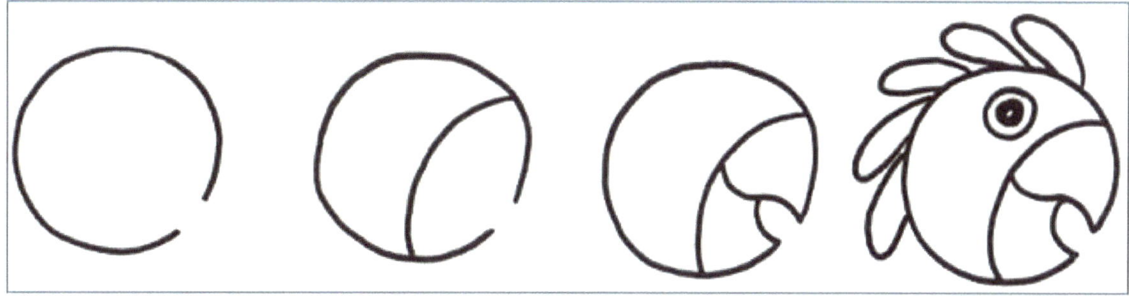

The parrot has the most varied tones. Have fun with the colors.

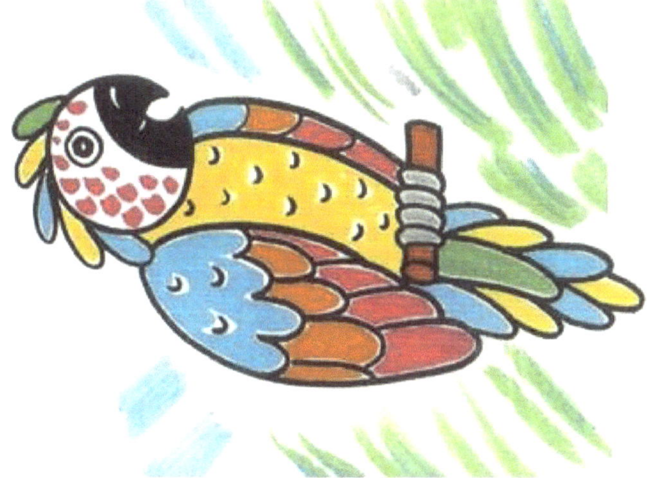

 **Trace over the blue lines of each model and then complete the drawing.**

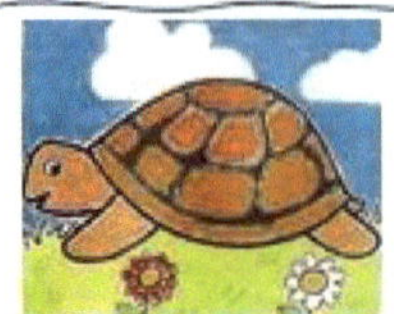

The turtle

Th turtle doesn't go very fast, so take your time to draw it. The shape of its scales can change, even when you see it from above!

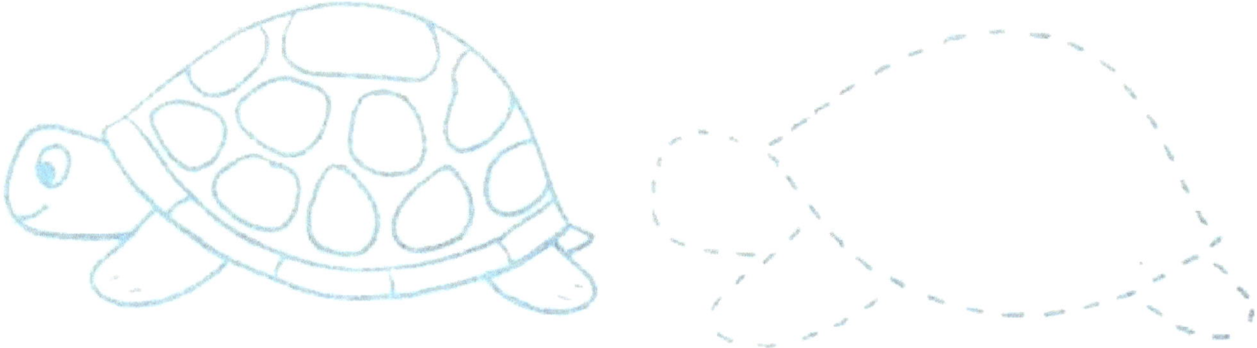

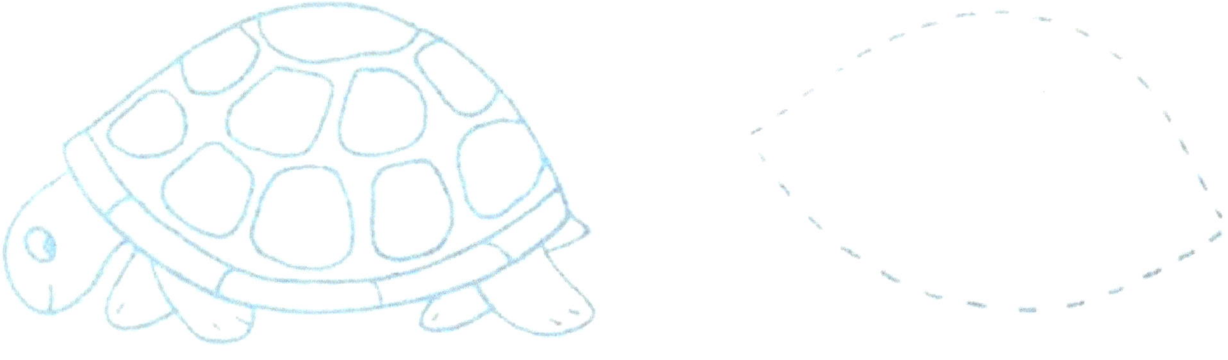

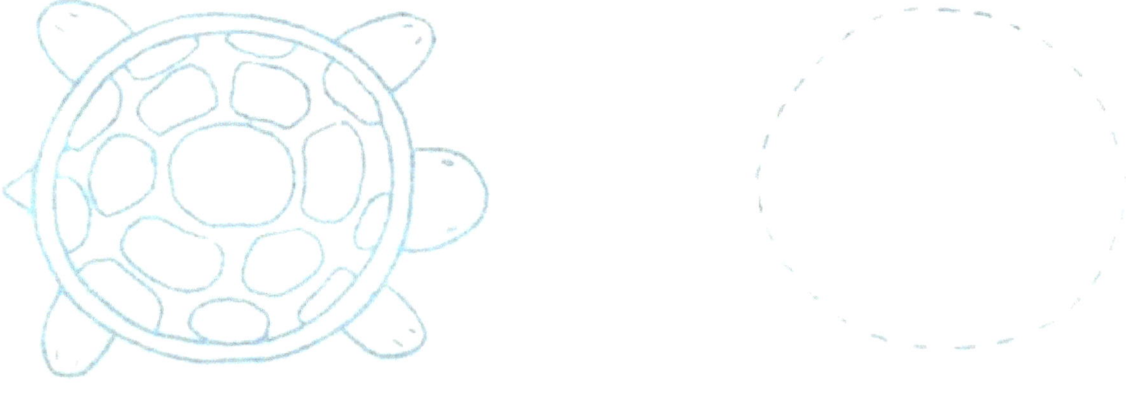

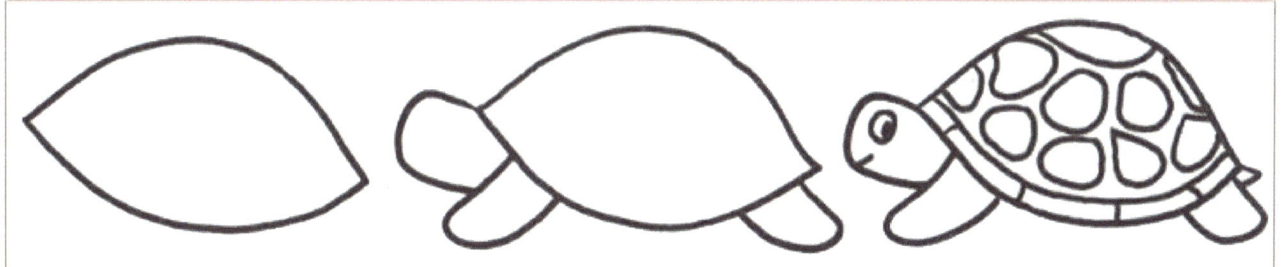

In order not to exceed with the pastels, leave a little white between the black line and the color.

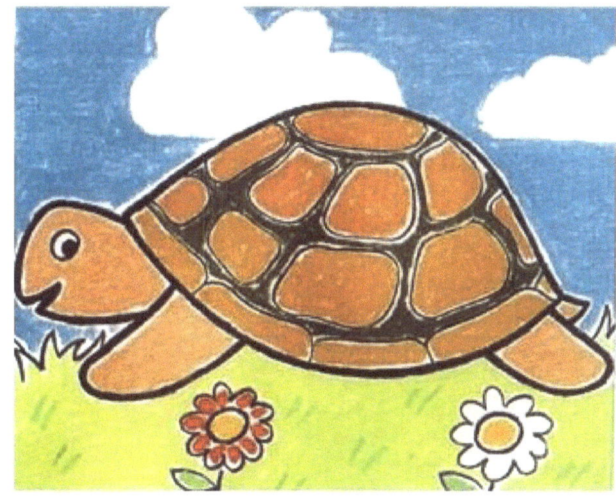

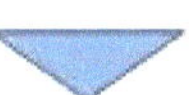 Trace over the blue lines of each model and then complete the drawing.

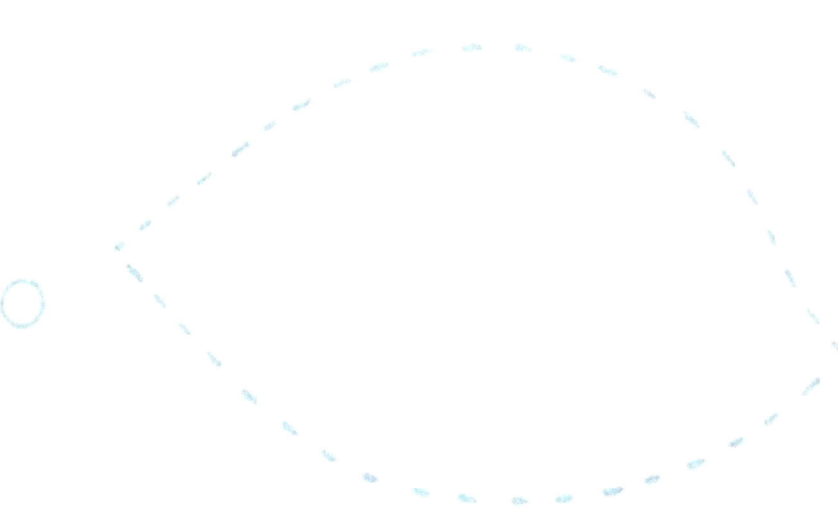

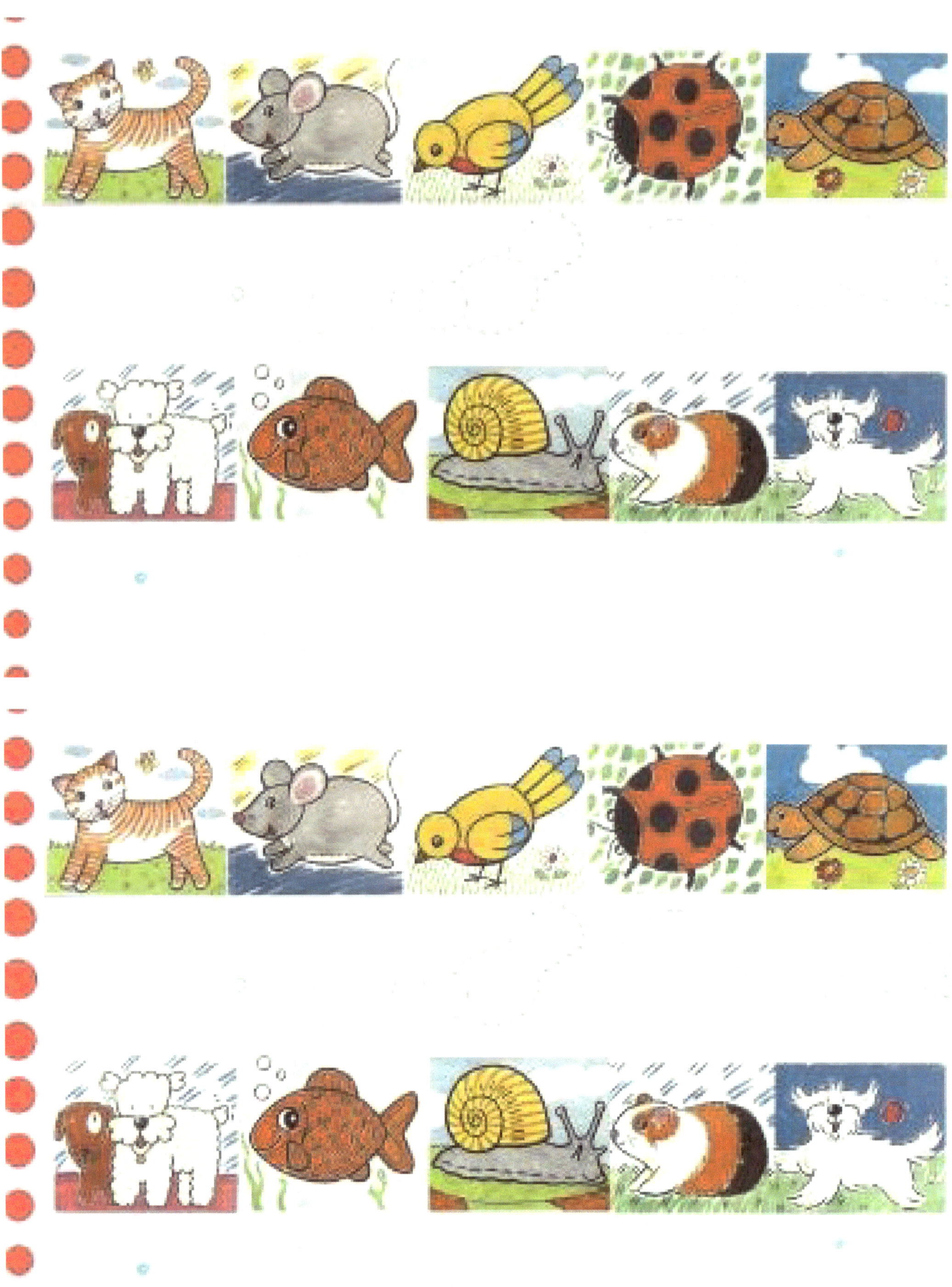